1e

C000233525

ukulele

... a handy beginner's guide!

Inside layout by Imesh Lemon
ISBN: 978-1-78305-459-6

HAL•LEONARD®

Visit Hal Leonard Online at
www.halleonard.com

Contact us:
Hal Leonard
7777 West Bluemound Road
Milwaukee, WI 53213
Email: info@halleonard.com

In Europe, contact:
Hal Leonard Europe Limited
42 Wigmore Street
Marylebone, London, W1U 2RY
Email: info@halleonardeurope.com

In Australia, contact:
Hal Leonard Australia Pty. Ltd.
4 Lentara Court
Cheltenham, Victoria, 3192 Australia
Email: info@halleonard.com.au

Introduction

This playbook will get you playing the ukulele in no time!

You'll learn the basic techniques you need, the essential chords and how to strum.

Let's get started!

Contents

Know your ukulele

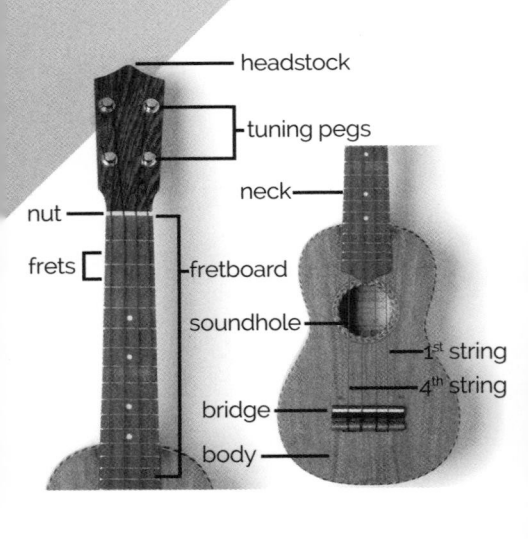

- headstock
- tuning pegs
- neck
- nut
- frets
- fretboard
- soundhole
- 1st string
- 4th string
- bridge
- body

Posture

A good posture leads to good technique, so it's worth taking a moment to make sure you're holding the ukulele correctly and—above all—comfortably.

Be sure to keep a straight back and relaxed shoulders.

Standing

For standing adopt an upright, balanced stance, with both feet firmly on the floor and shoulders straight. Support the uke by gently clasping it against your body. The right forearm holds the uke at about the bottom of the ribcage, against the right side of the stomach. The uke should stay in place without the need for the left arm.

Sitting

If you decide to sit, choose a seat that lets you keep a good upright posture. The right forearm should continue to hold the uke in position, but you might let the lap take a little of the weight as long as you don't let the position of the instrument 'sag' too much. Again, the left hand shouldn't take any of the weight.

Left-hand position

Whether standing or sitting, the left hand is there to fret the strings, and not to support the neck. Place the thumb around the back of the neck at the headstock end, as shown, without pressing or gripping. When you place the fingertips on the strings, it should take very little effort, and as long as you remember to clasp the uke with the right forearm, the left hand will be free to focus on fretting the strings.

Try sitting with a mirror in front of you to avoid craning your neck to see your fingers.

Tuning

Getting the ukulele in tune is a crucial skill.

There are various methods, but they all involve adjusting the pitch of the open (unfretted) strings by turning the tuning pegs to tighten or loosen each string until it sounds the correct note. You can choose a sound source to tune against, such as a piano, or a tuning fork; or else you can use an electronic tuner.

Below are the notes you need on the piano and the appropriate strings on the ukulele. The lowest-sounding string is tuned to the note known as middle C.

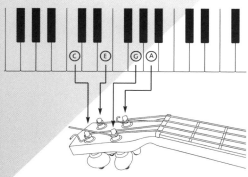

Relative tuning

If you tune the lowest string accurately, you can then use that string to tune the others. Here's how it works:

- Place a finger on the 7th fret of the C string—this will give you the note you need (G) to tune the open fourth string (also known as the bottom string).

- Once that's done, play a note on the 4th fret of C string. It'll be E, which is the note you need for the open second string.

- Finally, play a note on the 2nd fret of the fourth string to sound A, which is the note you'll need to tune the first string (the top string).

Check the diagram below for fret positions for each of the reference notes.

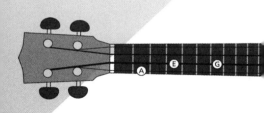

15

Electronic tuners

Using an electronic tuner has lots of advantages: they're pretty fool-proof, and very precise.

Play the A string, and the device will show you on its display whether you're pitched too low or high. Tune the string in the right direction and, when it's up to pitch, the display will let you know. Repeat with each string until the instrument is tuned.

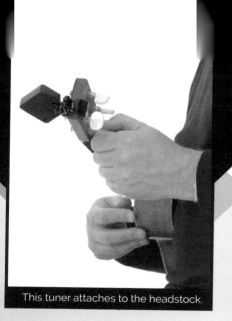

This tuner attaches to the headstock.

UKE LEGENDS

CLIFF EDWARDS

Cliff Edwards, also known as "Ukelele Ike" was an American singer and voice actor popular in the 1920-1930s. He took popular songs of the time and created new jazzy versions playing his soprano American Martin ukulele and scat singing his own inimitable syncopated versions. The popularity of the ukulele soared in the 1920s largely due to Edwards' influence. Sales of the instrument were in the millions and Tin Pan Alley publishers began adding ukulele chord diagrams to all their sheet music.

His biggest hit was with 'Singin' In The Rain' which reached No. 1 in the US in 1929. He voiced the character Jiminy Cricket and sang in the 1940 Disney film *Pinocchio*. His recording of the song was inducted into the Grammy Hall of Fame in 2002.

Essential tracks:
'I Can't Give You Anything But Love'
'Singin' In The Rain'
'I'll See You In My Dreams'

Chords

Uke players play chords, which are groups of notes strummed together. Chords are written down using chord diagrams, or chord boxes.

Here's how they look:

The thicker line at the top is the **nut**—the white plastic piece at the top of the ukulele neck.

The horizontal lines are **frets**.

The vertical lines are the **strings**, and the dots show where fingers are placed on the strings. If an O appears above a string, the string is played 'open': without any fingers on it.

Chord Diagrams

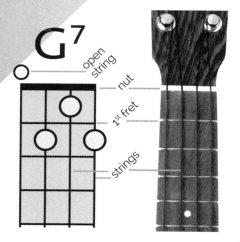

G⁷

open string

nut

1ˢᵗ fret

strings

Fingering chords

Let's take a close look at the way a single finger should sit on the fretboard. The fingertip should come down at right angles to the fretboard onto the string just behind the fretwire. If you find you're struggling to make a note sound without a huge effort, go back and check this basic finger position.

Your first chords

To start playing songs, you only need to know two chords, so let's make a start with C and G⁷.

Remember, the diagrams are shown upright, with the thick line at the top representing the nut—the piece at the top of the neck.

For now your right hand can simply curl up slightly and strum down across the strings. We'll get into some more advanced strumming soon, but for now just brush down with the thumb.

Try placing the 3rd finger on the 3rd fret of the first string. The fourth, third and second strings are open, and the first string only is fretted.

You're now fingering a C chord. If you brush down lightly across the strings with your right thumb, you'll hear the result.

All four strings should sound clearly. If the top string sounds a little muffled, or if the finger you're using on the top string is also touching another string, carefully adjust the position until you have the sound you're after.

Press the strings down as near as you can to the fret without them actually being on the fret. If you're pressing very hard to get a clear sound, there might be something a bit wrong with your finger position, so stop again and check that.

G⁷ chord

G⁷ uses three fingers on three different strings, so it's more involved than C.

Begin by placing the 1st finger on the 1st fret of the second string, and then place the 2nd and 3rd fingers either side, on the 2nd fret of the third and first strings. It might help to visualise the shape as a triangle.

Visualising shapes is a great way to remember the finger positions. You'll soon see that many shapes have similarities to each other, and knowing what these similarities are will be helpful when it comes to changing from one chord shape to another in quick succession.

G⁷

UKE LEGENDS

GEORGE FORMBY

In the UK the Lancashire comic singer George Formby played the ukulele early in his career but became more widely known for playing a 'banjo uke' or 'banjolele', a cross between a standard ukulele and the body of a banjo which produced a louder sound for unamplified performance. He was the highest paid entertainer in the UK during the thirties and forties with his often salty comic songs like 'When I'm Cleaning Windows' becoming very popular in the Second World War.

Formby's trademark was to play in a highly syncopated style, referred to as the "Formby style" featuring strumming patterns such as the 'split stroke', the 'triple', the 'fan', and the 'shake'. He would often keep several ukuleles tuned to different keys so he could interchange quickly for different songs in stage performances.

Essential tracks:
'Leaning On A Lampost'
'When I'm Cleaning Windows'
'Happy Go Lucky Me/
Banjo Boy'

Chord changes

Take a look at this piece of music: it's four 'bars' long, and alternates between the chord of C and G⁷. Play the exercise slowly through, and try to keep a steady beat.

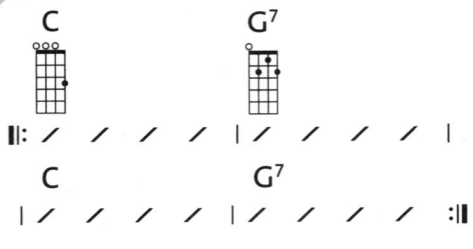

Strum down each time you see a slash (╱). Each slash represents a single beat of music.

Four strums of C will make a bar, and then it's time to play a bar of G^7.

The first few times, you might prefer to strum once on C, and count the four beats out while you change to G^7. Try to play the G^7 chord right at the beginning of the new bar. Count again and change back to C, and so on.

Once you have done it several times, you'll be able to strum slowly through, once on each beat without having to pause to change the shapes.

‖: :‖ These are repeat marks, and are found either side of a repeated section of music. In this case, they indicate simply that the whole of the music should be played again.

Starting to strum

Strumming is the most important technique to master on the ukulele, so it's worth looking at the basics before we go on and develop more advanced strumming styles. Strumming involves playing across all four strings together in a rhythmic fashion.

Previously, we simply strummed down on the first beat of each bar. Now we're going to start stringing strums together to create rhythms.

Let's look first at strumming on every beat. The correct strumming technique for this is to brush down across the strings with the back of the index finger. This is called the **down-strum**.

The hand should be held in front of the soundhole, with the other fingers tucked loosely in towards the palm, as shown. Use the wrist to create the movement, and brush gently across the strings in a single stroke. Try it using a C chord shape.

Quarter notes

Up till now we've used simple rhythm slashes to show the count, but in standard rhythm notation a stem is added to the note head to show that the note lasts for a beat.

This note value is called a quarter note (also known as a crotchet in the UK). The stem can point up or down, depending which is tidiest in the music.

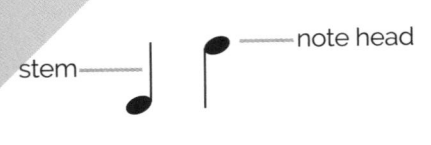

stem——

——note head

In strumming patterns where rhythm slashes are used, a stem is sometimes also added:

The quarter-note strums in the exercise on page 33 have their stems added.

New chord: F

The 1st finger is in the same position as for G⁷, with the 2nd finger on the 2nd fret of the bottom string:

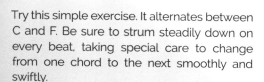

Try this simple exercise. It alternates between C and F. Be sure to strum steadily down on every beat, taking special care to change from one chord to the next smoothly and swiftly.

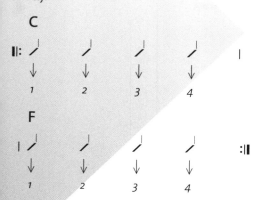

UKE LEGENDS

TINY TIM

A left-handed ukulele player, Tiny Tim was largely responsible for the resurgence of the ukulele's popularity in the 1960s. Interest in the Hawaiian instrument waned in the 1950s due to the emergence of rock 'n' roll but Tiny Tim (real name Herbert Khaury) and various other artists brought it back to the fore with a new quirky, comedic feel.

Tiny Tim would croon 1920's tunes with his signature falsetto alternating with his mellow baritone voice and accompanied by a ukulele he would produce from a paper grocery bag. He learned to play from a method book which accompanied his first Maccaferri Islander plastic ukulele endorsed by his favourite ukulele player, Arthur Godfrey.

Essential tracks:
'Tiptoe Through The Tulips With Me'
'Livin' In The Sunlight,
Lovin' In The Moonlight'
'I Got You, Babe'

Up-strum

Now let's think a little about what the hand does in between the down-strums.

In the previous exercise you may have noticed the right hand moves back into position immediately after the strum to begin the next strum. But when does it move? Just before the next strum? Right after the previous strum?

To play in the most relaxed, musical way, move the strumming hand back up right between the down-strums, exactly halfway through the beat. As you do so, brush the strings with the fingertip.

■ ■ ■ ■ ■ ■ ■

Here's how it would look.

The down strums are counted "1, 2, 3, 4" as before, but now there's an 'and'—shown with a + symbol—for the up-strums, too.

Count "1 and 2 and 3 and 4 and", strumming down, up, down, up, for a few bars, until you're comfortable with it.

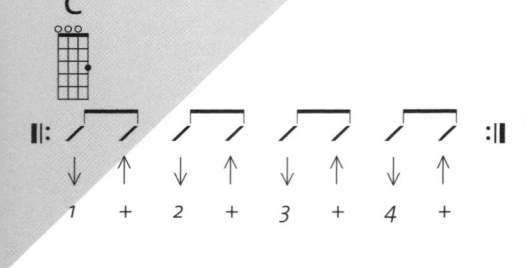

Eighth notes

In the exercise above there are eight strums in the bar, each worth half a beat. These notes are known as eighths (also called quavers in the UK), since there are 8 eighths in the bar. Where two eighths are played within one beat they are joined by a beam.

For some strumming rhythms the slashes now have tails and are joined in pairs indicating that each strum is worth half a beat. Two eighth notes make a quarter note.

Strumming patterns

Combining up-strums and down-strums in a rhythm builds a strumming pattern. Much of the energy in a song comes from the strumming pattern that accompanies it. Pretty much every strumming pattern we'll play using eighths requires the hand to strum down on the beat and up off the beat (between beats).

Try the following pattern. It uses eighths, but not on every possible eighth note. Sometimes the strums are allowed to ring on, which is indicated with the looped line joining notes together, known as a tie.

Make sure that your strumming hand keeps moving down and up in eighths even if it's not making contact with the strings every time. This way you'll be able to keep the beat and play the pattern smoothly.

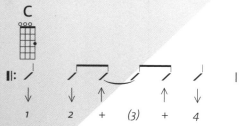

A tie ‿ is used to show that a note continues for the combined value of the connected notes.

New chords: C⁷, D⁷

Let's take a look at some seventh chords, which are a special kind of major chord. Firstly, C^7, which is very simple to play: the first finger is placed on the 1st fret of the first string, and that's it!

Also, here's D⁷. It uses the 2nd and 3rd fingers, on the 2nd fret of the fourth and second strings, respectively.

Now try putting these new shapes together with some you already know. As before, this exercise changes to a new chord on the first beat of each bar.

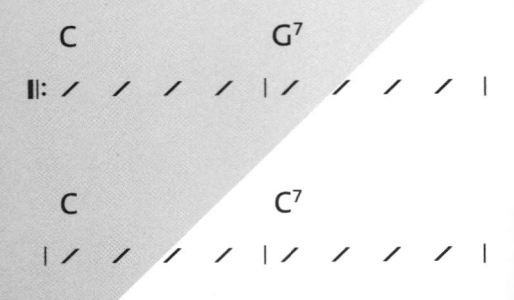

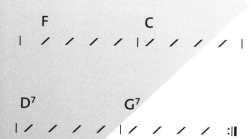

49

LYLE RITZ

Revered as the most influential jazz ukulele player in history, Lyle Ritz shaped the perception of the ukulele for an entire generation of uke musicians and teachers in Hawaii. Also a renowned session bassist, Ritz was part of the famous 'Wrecking Crew', a group of session artists who dominated the Hollywood studio scene in the 1960s.

Despite being famous for his bass playing skills, Ritz's most legendary work appeared on the two ukulele albums made at the very start of his career, *How About Uke?* (1957) and *50th State Jazz* (1959). Inducted into the Ukulele Hall of Fame and the Musicians Hall of Fame, he is hailed as a pioneer in the area of ukulele jazz.

Essential tracks:

'Tonight You Belong To Me' (from the film *The Jerk)*
'Polka Dots And Moonbeams'
'Fly Me To The Moon'

Swept strumming

A swept strum is just like a standard down-strum except that the strumming finger digs in a little to the strings, especially at the start of the stroke. As the stroke progresses, the movement is quite deliberate, sounding each string separately.

This strum is indicated by a wiggly arrow.

Try strumming down across the strings in turn, just slowly enough that each string can be heard one after the other, like a ripple. Allow the chord to ring on after each strum.

Sweep the finger over the strings

Try this rhythm, which should sound reminiscent of a tango beat.

The first strum is swept, with the other three played in the standard fashion. Be sure to start the swept strum early.

Notice also the accent (>), indicating that the swept strum should be emphasised.

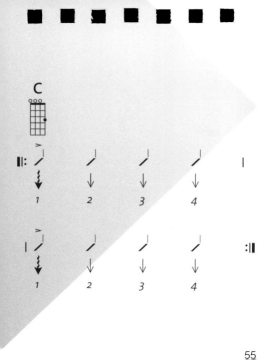

UKE LEGENDS

GEORGE HARRISON

Though mostly known for his prowess on the guitar, the 'quiet Beatle' George Harrison was also a skilled and passionate ukulele player. A huge fan of George Formby and a member of the Ukulele Society of Great Britain, Harrison performed on and was pictured with a ukulele for his acclaimed solo album *All Things Must Pass*.

He plays an outstanding solo in the style of Formby on the track 'Free As A Bird' including some of 'When I'm Cleaning Windows' in the closing bars.

Essential tracks:
'Between The Devil And
The Deep Blue Sea'
'Free As A Bird'

Reading tablature

For strumming chords, diagrams showing left-hand finger positions are sufficient.

But when it comes to finger picking, uke players use a more complete notation system. This is tablature, or tab.

Tablature is a musical notation system for stringed instruments that shows the performer exactly where to play each note on the fretboard.

The tablature system consists of four horizontal lines (a staff), each representing a ukulele string. The staff generally has a 'TAB' clef at the beginning of the staff.

The G string is the bottom line of the tablature staff, and the A string is the top line. This layout is inverted from the actual string positions on the instrument. The string that in reality is closest to the ground is shown at the top, whereas the bottom line is shown uppermost.

A number on a line indicates at which fret to depress that string. This example shows various strings fretted or open (0).

Sometimes, the stems and beams above or below the staff denote the rhythm. In this example, the rhythm is a combination of eighth notes and quarter notes.

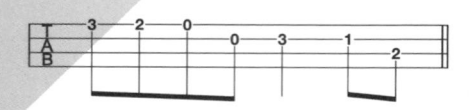

Finger picking

Instead of strumming chords, with all the strings played at the same time, uke players also pick the strings individually with the fingers and thumb. This is known as finger picking. As with strumming, finger picking is played in patterns—repeated sequences. Tablature is ideal to show all the details for finger picking patterns.

Let's take a look at some fundamentals.

To pick the strings, use the nails or fingertips, depending on the sound you're after—and the strength of your nails!

The thumb plays the bottom string, with the index, ring and middle fingers playing the other three strings as shown. Some players like to place the little finger on the front of the uke to help keep the picking hand steady.

Finger picking

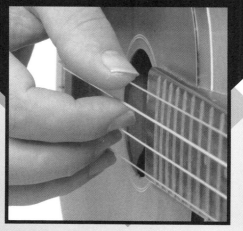

Take a look at the picking pattern below. It uses all four strings, as most patterns do, and with the shapes shown the notes of the chord are played in order of pitch, making it an ideal pattern for simple, unobtrusive accompaniment.

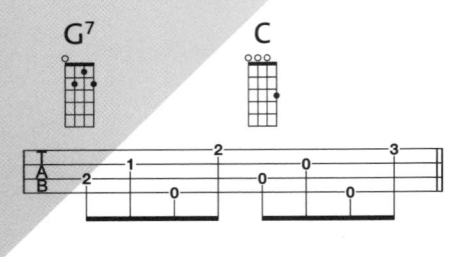

Try this simple pattern, which again uses all four strings. In the fourth part of the pattern, the first and fourth strings are played simultaneously. The pattern then repeats.

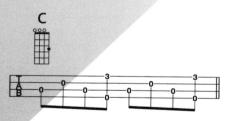

UKE LEGENDS

ISRAEL 'IZ' KAMAKAWIWO'OLE

Israel "Iz" Kamakawiwo'ole is a relative newcomer on the ukulele scene but his influence on the recent resurgence of the instruments popularity cannot be denied. His cover version medley combining 'Over The Rainbow' and 'What A Wonderful World' (1997) became synonymous with the ukulele in the mainstream.

His lilting, relaxed recording has been featured in countless films and TV programs since and has become a staple request for ukulele students. Israel's style included fusing his Hawaiian heritage with jazz and reggae music featuring the Hawaiian instrument and his own vocals. His album *Facing Future* is the bestselling album of all time by a Hawaiian artist.

Essential tracks:
'Somewhere Over The Rainbow/
What A Wonderful World'
'Hawaii '78'

Finger picking continued

It's common to finger pick in eighth notes: two picks per beat. This creates an interesting texture without being too cluttered. If the tempo of the song is fast, however, it might be enough just to pick one note on every beat. Experiment by accenting certain notes of the pattern.

If you emphasise the on beats, you'll find the pattern sounds a little more solid—but overdo it and it'll become a bit too predictable. On the other hand, accenting some of the off beats can create syncopation, which will make the pattern sound more jazzy and lively.

This pattern is made of four repeating eighth notes. Practise the pattern until it sounds smooth and relaxed.

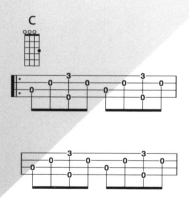

New chord: Dm

The 'm' stands for minor, a type of chord that some people describe as having a darker or more sombre sound than the other type we've looked at, which are major chords.

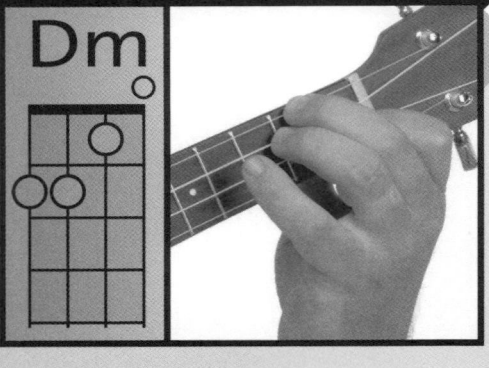

Sixteenth notes

Some rhythms contain notes that last half as long as an eighth note. These are sixteenth notes, written with an extra flag on the stem. In the UK they are called **semiquavers**.

As with eighth notes, they can be joined together with beams. Four sixteenths make up a quarter note.

The following exercise has sixteenth notes in it. Try playing it through on the D minor chord, putting greater emphasis on the accented notes at each '+'.

Notice the way the sixteenths are counted: "1 e + a, 2 e + a" etc.

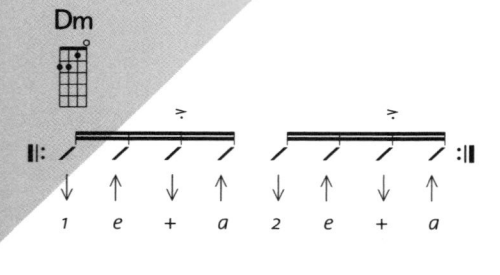

Chord library

C

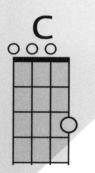

G^7

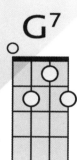

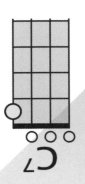

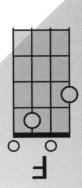

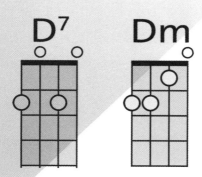

75

What you've learnt:

- how to handle and tune the ukulele
- six essential chords
- how to read chord diagrams and tablature
- strumming and picking patterns
- basic rhythmic notation

Now it's time to find some of your favourite songs to learn to play! Look for ukulele tab music or lead-sheets with chord boxes to learn from. You might like to use the **Music Playbook Ukulele Chords** as a reference for any chords you may find unfamiliar.

Learning more

To learn more about playing the ukulele and add more songs to your repertoire, try these titles:

- **Absolute Beginners: Ukulele** (Book/CD) AM991804
- **Mike Jackson: Uke'n Play Supa Easy Ukulele** (Book/CD) AM1001781
- **Strumalong Ukulele: Beatles Hits** (Book/CD) NO9154
- **The Little Black Book Of Classic Songs For Ukulele** (Book) AM1006423

Recommended listening

Now that you've got to grips with the fundamentals of ukulele playing, try listening to how the professionals do it!

The songs listed below all feature classic ukulele parts; some are more difficult than others, but armed with the basic techniques you've learnt in this playbook, you should soon be able to approach some of them.

'Somewhere Over The Rainbow/
What A Wonderful World' (Israel
Kamakawiwo'ole)

'While My Guitar Gently Weeps' (Jake
Shimabukuro)

'Ain't She Sweet' (The Beatles)

'Hey, Soul Sister' (Train)

'Tonight You Belong To Me' (from the
film *The Jerk* recorded by Lyle Ritz)

'Ukulele Lady' (Vaughn De Leath)

'Tiptoe Through The Tulips' (Tiny Tim)

'Leaning On A Lampost' (George
Formby)

'Good Company' (Brian May)

'That's My Weakness Now'
(Cliff 'Ukulele Ike' Edwards)

'Miss Dy-nami-tee'
(the Ukulele Orchestra of Great Britain)

MORE IN THE Playbook SERIES